God Never Slept

God Never Slept

Sharon Simonsen

Pacific Press Publishing Association
Mountain View, California
Oshawa, Ontario

Cover and design by Paul B. Ricchiuti

Library of Congress Cataloging in Publication Data

Simonsen, Sharon.
God never slept.

(Daybreak series)
1. Simonsen, Sharon. 2. Simonsen, Alan.
3. Converts, Seventh-day Adventist—United States—Biography.
I. Title.
BX6191.S55   248.2'4   [B]   81-22451
ISBN O-8163-0472-6   AACR2

Acknowledgment

First of all I would like to thank a very patient and loving husband who has stuck through an awful lot with me. Then I'd like to say thank you to two beautiful little Christians—my children, Sondra and Derek.

To the man who lead us to the Lord and brought us through some tough times, Mike Jones and his family.

To two very special friends. First is Alice Rogers, our neighbor and friend, the one that led us to Mike and to the Seventh-day Adventist Church. If it hadn't been for her and her friend, I don't know where we would be today. Thanks, Alice. Second is Doris, carefree, beautiful Doris. She befriended me right from the very beginning and has been through an awful lot with me, but always kept me close to the Lord.

A special thanks to Mort Juberg, editor of the North Pacific Union *Gleaner,* for all his help in editing my work. Thanks, Mort. I couldn't have done it without you!

Last, but most important, is the Lord! All I can say is that if it weren't for Him, there would be no story. I do thank You, praise You, and love You, Lord! Never once did you get tired of my backsliding. Thank You for always being there when I needed you and even when I didn't know I needed you.

Introduction

Have you ever thought of the times when things happened you couldn't explain?

Have you ever thought you just couldn't live or make it through another day, but you did?

Have you ever stopped to think of the number of times the Lord has been working with you, even when you didn't ask?

Have you ever stopped to think of the times the door of commitment has been opened for you to walk through if you wanted to?

I used to think a lot about these things and have questioned them, but I only recently found the way to the door—the door of total commitment to the Lord.

To give totally of yourself is the most difficult thing anyone can do, especially when you are used to thinking of yourself first. To let go of that selfishness and accept the responsibility that comes with that commitment was the hardest battle I had.

I had to learn to accept people the way they are, especially those who were closest to me. I had to stop worrying about what they are or are not doing that doesn't please me.

I had to work on myself first. Then I had a better attitude toward others.

When I stop and think of it now, I guess most of my life I have been searching and didn't realize it.

You know the feeling! The emptiness inside that makes you search and search for that someone or something to fill the big empty space.

Actually, all I had to do was reach out. My Saviour was there all the time just waiting for me to finally say, "Dear Lord, I am yours. I can't do it on my own. I am nothing without You. Please take my heart, soul, mind, body, and spirit—all of me, dear Lord—and strengthen me. Use me to Your advantage to help others. I need to be used, needed, and loved. Dear Lord, I know through You all things are possible."

I claimed several of my favorite Bible promises: "Fear thou not; for I am with thee: be not dismayed; for I am thy God: I will strengthen thee; yea, I will help thee; yea, I will uphold thee with the right hand of my righteousness." Isaiah 41:10. "I sought the Lord, and he heard me, and delivered me from all my fears." Psalm 34:4. "Delight thyself also in the Lord; and he shall give thee the desires of thine heart." Psalm 37:4. "Therefore I say unto you, What things soever ye desire, when ye pray, believe that ye receive them, and ye shall have them." Mark 11:24.

These promises have meant so very much to me, especially during my early Christian growth. You have to believe these promises, and believe the Bible as the book of truth. Then totally put your faith in the Lord.

There is no earthly thing in this world that measures up to the joys and excitement that the Lord gives anyone who will just *reach out* and *take Him* at His word. How thankful I am that God never slept.

If you do this I can personally guarantee that with Him and His strength you can go through any crisis or do anything you want, *if it is His will.*

Chapter One

Alan stood outside in the backyard. I could see him from the kitchen window as I prepared dinner and glanced out occasionally across the valley. It was one of those beautiful, clear, sunny days in southern California, and I hummed as I worked.

Suddenly the kitchen door slammed. I turned to see Alan come into the kitchen with a troubled look on his face.

"Hurry with the dinner, and get the kids to bed as early as possible. I want to talk to you," he said.

Now I knew why he had had more than his usual amount to drink that day. He had something important to say, and he felt he needed some additional courage. Immediately I stopped humming. I felt my body becoming numb and then flushed. I guess I knew what was coming.

"All right," I agreed, but my voice couldn't help quavering a bit. Nervously I went about finishing dinner preparations. We ate, only the children seeming to be oblivious to the tension. I did the dishes and then hurried the children off to bed, tucking them in absentmindedly.

In the kitchen once more, Alan and I sat down at the kitchen table. We looked nervously into each other's eyes for what seemed an eternity. I noticed tears forming in Alan's eyes. He fought them away and then, with his hands tightly clenched on the table in front of him, he spoke.

"I want a divorce. I don't love you anymore. I don't know that I ever really loved you. Maybe we got married too young. The kids are in my way. I—I don't love them either. I'm leaving. I want out. That's final. I just want out!"

I sat there stunned. I thought of the summer in Maine when Alan and I had first met. It was during the summer vacation just before our senior year in high school. We were young, impressionable, and fell in love with the thought of being in love, I guess.

We had come from totally different backgrounds. Alan came from a fairly strict Baptist family in Massachusetts. I came from a Catholic family in New Hampshire.

We had dated for three years after meeting that first summer. We became engaged, but broke the engagement three times before our marriage in July of 1967. We had had so many religious differences that our marriage seemed doomed to fail. Alan refused to raise any children we might have as Catholics because he didn't believe in the teachings of the Catholic Church.

As a child I had had all sorts of questions about God, but since I had been told to believe, I had done so blindly. However, I finally decided to leave my religion for the sake of our relationship. After all, I reasoned, I wasn't leaving God, just a religion.

Within three years of our wedding we had two children, a daughter, Sondra, and a son, Derek.

Shortly after Derek was born, Alan's company transferred him to Pittsburgh, Pennsylvania. While living there I decided to join the Baptist Church. On the way home from church after my baptism, we stopped at a store for some cigarettes and beer. We reasoned that all Baptists drank and smoked—but not in front of each other. That was how we rationalized what we did. We couldn't understand how anyone could have fun without drinking or smoking.

Fourteen months after arriving in Pittsburgh, Alan received a notice of a transfer to California. He learned that if he did not take the job, he would have to leave the company. What were we going to do?

We had already discovered that things were not going well between us. We had just been existing together with no strong feelings. Since Alan had to leave within two weeks for a company meeting in California and to decide whether he would take the job or not, it was decided that I should fly home to visit my parents, take the children with me, and do a lot of serious thinking about our life together. We were both to do some thinking about our marriage. Did we want to make it work? Would I go to California and make the best of things?

After being separated for a week and doing some soul-searching, we both decided to try to make a go of our marriage. I was a little afraid of going out to California and being so far from my family, but both Alan and I decided we had too much invested together in life to toss it aside now.

We went to California where we found a beautiful home. Before long we were living like the typical southern Californian. However, shortly after getting settled, unpleasant things started to happen. Many nights Alan didn't come home until early morning. This happened time and time again. Our marriage simply existed. But I knew it couldn't last like that. So the night when Alan confronted me about a divorce, down deep I had expected it.

"I love you, but I can't bear to be married to someone that doesn't love me," I said to Alan. "I want nothing more than for you to be happy. And if you are not happy here—then—you—you—should leave." The words were out. But they weren't really my words. The Lord must have been giving me strength. Normally I wouldn't have acted this way at all.

Alan went into the bedroom to pack. When he came out with his suitcase in hand, he set it down and jokingly said, "I left you the good hair dryer."

He seemed to hesitate then and look about the room. "Why doesn't he leave?" I thought.

As if in answer to my thought, Alan said, "I don't want to leave you alone like this. I'll ask the neighbors to come over and sit with you for a while."

Our neighbors were out. Alan called several places trying to locate them. When he found them he told them he was leaving me, and he hoped they would come over and stay with me for a while.

I couldn't understand why, if he didn't love me, he was so concerned about leaving me alone. Why did he stay until the neighbors arrived?

The next morning at seven o'clock Alan called on the telephone. "I'm sorry," he said. "I made a mistake. I didn't mean what I said. May I come home and talk?"

I felt emotionally and physically exhausted from the night before. Besides I didn't feel we could really talk because now the children had come into my bedroom, so I suggested that he come over after Sondra had gone to school. I said I'd get the neighbors to watch Derek. Then we could talk freely.

When Alan arrived, we sat down at the kitchen table. "I know I am not an easy person to live with. I know that I have made a lot of mistakes in my life, but I can't turn my emotions off and on that easily after the way you hurt me last night," I said.

Since he had to go out of town on a business trip that couldn't be postponed, he wanted my answer about getting together again before he left. "Could we possibly start over again?" he asked.

I couldn't make a decision that fast. "I need some time to think," I said. So we parted, not knowing just what would happen to us.

While Alan was away, I decided to see a marriage counselor. I knew that Alan was a firm believer that people should handle their own problems and not air them with strangers. But I felt I had to talk with someone about our problem.

When Alan returned and asked for my decision, I said, "Before I make a final decision about taking you back, you have to agree to go with me to the mental health center for counseling." By the look on his face I knew what he was thinking. But he agreed at last.

"OK, I'll go, but I don't think there's any reason for it, and I think the whole idea is stupid."

By the end of the session I had decided myself that these sessions were going to get us nowhere. However, I finally decided to take Alan back and try again.

I started going to church with some friends of mine every week. The closer I got to the Lord the more I began to realize that Alan had a drinking problem.

I had really enjoyed our parties and drinking. But I didn't drink day after day the way Alan did.

"Please get some help. You have a real problem!" I would beg him, but he wouldn't listen to me.

He didn't go to church anymore, but I was determined to continue to go. I didn't know much about God or the Bible, but I did know I felt a strange sense of peace and security when at church.

Our next move took us to Oregon after we had lived in California for two years. We continued our usual life-style of partying and drinking and smoking. We would be at a party or off in our own little make-believe world of drinking, smoking cigarettes and a little marijuana as well.

True, the life-style in Oregon was much slower paced than what we had grown used to in California, but we still found excuses to drink and party. And Alan drank more than he ever had before.

I realized that I, too, was beginning to drink quite a bit on my own. Having basically a weak character, I blamed Alan for my drinking. But now I know it was my own fault, and my way of dealing with a situation I couldn't cope with was to lay the blame on another.

"Alan, please, do something about your drinking! It is starting to scare me. I wish you would admit to having a problem for the sake of our marriage." I tried to convince him, but as far as he was concerned there still was no problem, even though it had now been about eight years since he'd gone a day without a drink.

"Please, at least think about it a little for me," I begged him.

I was getting scared because of my own drinking, and I was beginning to hate him for his. I was also tired of making excuses to the children for all the broken promises he kept making to them. I was tired of trying to make him look good to them all the time.

Our partying continued, and when Alan was gone on one of his business trips I spent the time deciding that when he got back I would ask him for a divorce.

I talked to my boss, who was a level-headed fellow. He said, "I think you're making a big decision too fast. If Alan and you have made it for almost eleven years, you must have something going for you. You should give serious thought to what you're planning to do."

I did decide to wait for a while. And then something happened which began to change our lives completely.

One night as Alan and I were sitting in the living room, we heard a knock on the front door. I opened the door to find a woman standing there with a loaf of homemade bread in her hand and a smile on her face.

"Hi," she said, "I'm Alice Rogers, your new neighbor. We just moved in across the street, and I thought I'd introduce myself to you."

"Why don't you come in," I invited, stepping back from the door and motioning her in.

"I brought you some homemade zucchini bread," she said. "I feel it's a good way to break the ice when meeting new friends."

I thanked her for her thoughtfulness, and then asked, "Are you from Oregon?"

"No," she laughed, "from California. But do I hear a faint accent when you speak? Where are you from?"

"Originally from Boston," I said. "Actually I come from a small town just outside of Boston. I always say Boston though. If you haven't lived there, you wouldn't know the little town where I'm from."

Alice persisted. "Where did you actually live? I lived in a little town called Stoneham, and I worked in the New England Memorial Hospital for three years. I just might know the little town where you lived."

"What?" I gasped. "You lived in Stoneham?" I couldn't believe my ears. "Stoneham is where I am from. I grew up there and graduated from the Stoneham High School. I—I can't believe this. Imagine having someone move in right across the road that lived in the same town that I grew up in!"

That set the pace for an evening of conversation that made us instant friends. We learned we had much in common.

Alice and her friend, accepted Alan and me from the beginning. They never made us feel uncomfortable or said anything about our drinking or smoking. They accepted us for what we were.

A few months after we met Alice, we found out that she was a Seventh-day Adventist. We didn't know much about her religion, but never asked either. Alice never mentioned her faith or tried to push it on us. She just set a good Christian example being there when we needed her, never judging us, never putting us down for the way we lived—and she loved us the way we were!

One day when I told Alice what I planned to do about my marriage, she said, "Sharon, I think you're making too big a decision too fast. Don't you think you could maybe talk first instead of going through with these divorce plans?"

"No, I don't think so, Alice. This has been going on for too long now."

"I wish you would reconsider. I wish I could get you to talk to a man I know. His name is Jones, Mike Jones."

At that time I still was totally convinced that I was doing the right thing. "I am going to ask Alan for a divorce when he comes home," I said. "I have to pick him up at the airport when he returns in a couple weeks."

Chapter Two

The man Alice wanted us to talk to was a Seventh-day Adventist minister.

"You've got to be kidding," I said when I learned that. "First of all, I have my mind made up, and second, what would a Seventh-day Adventist minister want with us?"

Without any hesitation Alice said, "He could just listen and maybe help you. From what I've heard he's had a lot of problems too and really relates well to people!"

"We're not of his faith, and he's probably busy with people of his own religion and of his own church," I told her.

Alice mentioned the minister to me a few times during the two weeks that followed, but I didn't want to hear about him or anything that might keep my marriage together.

The day of Alan's return home, I was scared. To give myself a little courage I drank two or three beers before I left for the airport. I took my time getting there and pulled up in front of the terminal and waited in the van. I always dropped Alan off in front of the airport when he left on a trip and later picked him up there.

Now I waited and waited.

He finally came out of the terminal, and I got out of the van. "Where were you?" he asked. "I thought you'd be inside waiting. Where are the kids?"

"The kids are at home. I'm sorry but I always wait out here for you; I didn't think you'd be waiting inside for me," I said.

Alan got in on the driver's side, and I got in beside him. Then he told me he had been waiting inside and couldn't imagine where I was. He thought I'd bring the kids. We'd be waiting for him with open arms at the gate. Instead when he arrived there was no one to greet him, and he watched the other people around him being greeted by their loved ones and wondered where we were.

He reached out then to put his arms around me and he kissed me. I just sat there in the car and gave him a brief little peck on the cheek in return.

He seemed to sense then that something was wrong, but what? He started the van and we headed home. While he drove he said, "Look in the suitcase; there's a present there for you."

In his suitcase I found five grams of solid gold in a bar shape on a chain.

"Oh, how beautiful! Thank you, Alan. But you didn't have to spend that much money. It must have cost an awful lot," I said as I started to choke up. But I decided I couldn't give in now. I had this all planned. I wouldn't back out.

I could tell he was exhausted, and he just wanted to get home and see the kids. But I suggested that we go to the river for a while "I want to talk to you before we get home," I said.

He glanced at me questioningly, but said, "OK."

I had never been so cold, selfish, hard, and without

feelings as I was that night. We drove up to a special spot, and Alan turned off the engine.

We sat there for a short period in total silence; then I blurted out, "I don't love you anymore, and I want a divorce! That is that. I don't want to talk about it anymore either. My mind is made up."

After a stunned silence Alan started to cry. "No, you can't have a divorce," he sobbed. "I love you and the kids. I'll fight for the kids; you can't have them." He clenched his fingers around the steering wheel.

Now I was getting angry and said, "No, you won't. The kids always stay with the mother."

"Is there someone else?" he asked.

"No. I have just had it with the way we've been living. Drinking, smoking, partying—bills and more bills and no kind of security. I just can't take it anymore and I want out."

We silently drove home. I praise God for being with us that night. I got the kids to bed, and Alan and I talked until around three in the morning. Alan finally said, "Well, I love you and won't let you go. Please stay with me."

All I could say was, "I can't stay with you and your drinking any longer."

I was tired of all the drinking. But drinking had gotten to be about the only way I could stand Alan or his breath when he'd come home after an evening with his friends. I was tired of his wanting the best of everything even if we couldn't afford it, coming and going whenever he wanted, and I was tired of making him look good to the children.

"You have to do some serious thinking because I'm not going to budge!" I said.

That was May 20, 1978. The very next day when Alan got up he called Alcoholics Anonymous. When I got up he told me that two men were coming over to talk with him about A.A.

I wondered about Alan's sincerity, but I went along with it. Why, I don't know, but I did.

The men from A.A. came and talked to both of us for about four hours, and Alan agreed to go to an A.A. meeting the next night. One of the fellows promised to pick him up. I was grateful for that because I knew that Alan couldn't back out. That's a start, I thought.

The next day I got up and left for work before Alan got up, but felt I should call him and let him know I was OK.

"Would you like to go to lunch with me?" he asked. "Thanks again for calling me," he added, apparently grateful for my call.

"Yes, I'd like to go. It would give us more time to talk. Come around noon. Thank you," I said.

We were at a very polite stage in our relationship.

Alan took me to one of my favorite restaurants for lunch. We were both upset and still uncomfortable with each other, so it was difficult to make small talk. After all, we had destroyed the faith and trust in each other that we had had.

After lunch we went back to where I worked, and I told my boss that Alan and I needed time to talk, "Can I please have the rest of the afternoon off?"

"Naturally, you can have the afternoon off, as long as you can get things straightened out," my boss said.

So Alan and I left and found another place along the river to sit and talk. After a long talk we decided that we would like to try again. We realized that we must deeply love one another since after all we'd put each other through in our almost eleven years of marriage, we still seemed to want each other and still wanted to try to make a go of it.

"I feel like we're all talked out and we need to talk to someone else," Alan said. Then he added quickly, "I think the only way we can make a go of it this time is if we have Jesus in our lives."

"You know, I think you're right," I agreed. "But we'll both have to go to church and get close to God, or it won't work," I said.

We drove around and tried to find a church that was open so we could talk to a minister. We were desperate to talk to someone!

Then I remembered what Alice had said about the minister she called Mike Jones. We stopped at a gas station, and I called her at the Adventist hospital where she worked. I briefly explained to her what was going on. She took the phone number from where we were calling and said that she'd call right back as soon as she was able to set something up.

We waited right there until she called back.

"I was unable to reach Mike Jones," she said, "but I was able to talk to the chaplain at the hospital, and he'll be glad to talk to you."

I said, "Thanks, Alice. Tell him we'll be right over."

Meeting that chaplain was amazing. We found he wasn't any different to talk to than to a minister of any other faith. We had decided before we got there to try and get the most out of what he'd say, even though he was a Seventh-day Adventist. He was still a worker for the Lord.

Pastor Bob Babcock did indeed give us some beneficial information and ideas on how to be considerate and let each other know that we were thinking of each other.

After visiting with us he asked, "Would you mind if I had prayer with you before you leave?"

We both looked at each other, and Alan said, "No, we wouldn't! We'd appreciate it very much."

After prayer we thanked him and left feeling confident of the new way we were going about things, our new attitude toward each other, and the beginning of a newfound relationship with the Lord. This time, we felt, we were sharing!

Alice called that night to find out how things had gone and said, "I'm happy that you found someone to talk to, but I'd still like you to talk to Mike Jones."

"If you think he'll want to talk to us and will have the time, we'd love to," I told her.

She promised she would try to reach him and get back to us.

We later found out that when Alice called Mike Jones, he said, "I am really too busy with the people in my church to be involved with anyone else. However, pray about it, and if you are really impressed by the Lord that I should talk to them, call me back, and I'll talk to them."

She did pray about it. Then she asked me if I was sure we wanted to talk to him.

I replied emphatically, "Yes!"

Alice called Mike back and told him she felt convicted that he should talk to us. She gave him our phone number before she hung up.

Later when the phone rang and I answered, Mike Jones was on the line. "I've been talking to Alice Rogers and heard that you and your husband would like to talk to me. You would like some guidance and counseling," he said.

I began to tell him a little of what had been going on in our lives. But he cut me off by saying, "I'll talk to you both about things later. Let's set up a time when we can meet."

When a day and time had been agreed upon, he hung up.

"He sure was crabby!" I thought to myself.

I later learned what an extremely busy person he was. I also learned that he liked to see people's eyes when he talked to them and didn't care to discuss important matters over the phone.

We met with Mike Jones on June 5. He was a little older than Alan and I, but he was just a regular-looking person.

Alan and I thought our story was so unusual and complicated that we'd surprise or shock him for sure. But Pastor Mike patiently sat and listened while we told him our story. We both noticed he didn't seem the least bit shocked.

"Now I'd like to share with you my story," he said.

We could hardly believe our ears. His story was almost like hearing ours all over again!

Imagine meeting a minister that has had some problems! A minister who would admit to them. Alan and I found it easy to relate to Mike; we had something in common with him, and he understood what we were going through! I had never met a minister like him.

Why, all ministers I'd ever met would never let their guard down like that or even admit any faults. They wanted to appear too good or saintly for that!

Needless to say, we liked him right away and got a big spiritual lift from him. He didn't even judge us, condemn us, or say, "You're going to hell for that!"

All he did was show us love and understanding, and have faith in us that if we would stay close to the Lord, he had confidence that we'd make it.

Mike started calling us every so often on the phone. He'd stop over with books for us to read or just to ask us how we were doing.

Mike, like Alice, never mentioned his religion or tried to push it on us; he was just interested in us as God's children. He did, however, mention once that if we would like to study the Bible, he would be glad to get some studies together and help us. We said that it sounded great and we'd think about it. Soon after this we left for an East Coast vacation.

We hadn't been home in Oregon again for more than a few days when Mike appeared at our front door. "I received your postcard and thought I'd stop by and see how you've been doing," he said.

We told him all about our vacation and all the events that took place while we were there.

We visited for a while, and then Mike asked, "Have you had a chance to think about whether you want Bible studies? The reason I'm asking is that I know another couple that wants to study too!"

Alan and I looked at each other. Alan gave me a nod of his head, and I said, "Yes, we would like to have Bible studies. Whenever the other couple would like to start will be fine with us."

Mike suggested we decide on a night that would be best for us. "I'll check with the other couple and get back to you," he said before he left.

In a couple of weeks we started our Bible studies on a Monday night. Alan and I had been talking about wanting to give up smoking for many months and happened to mention it the night of our Bible study.

Mike answered immediately, "There is a new Five-Day Plan starting soon, and if you are really interested in stopping smoking I'll find out about it for you."

"Yes, we really need to stop!" I said. "We've been talking about it a lot lately. Naturally, the main reason is because we know it's not good for us, and second is the money! We figured out how much we spend a year, and it's staggering."

The next week at Bible-study time Mike said, "I found out the next program starts in two weeks, but it's the television one. You'll be on television all week."

We weren't too impressed with the idea of being on television for a whole week, but decided if we were going to stop smoking, right then was a good time.

"We've decided to go ahead with it," we told Mike. "If you want to make the arrangements for us, we'd appreciate it."

We smoked incessantly for two weeks—right until we opened the door of the television studio that first night.

During the week Mike checked with Harold Burden, the man in charge of the program, to see how we were doing. He also called Alan and me one evening and asked how we were doing.

"We're trying, Mike. So far we haven't had a cigarette; all we can do is keep trying," I told him.

"Keep up the good work. I'm really proud of you two. Just remember, we're all behind you and are praying for you! I'll check with you later."

Harold Burden now knew that we were friends of Mike and that he was counseling us. Mike had told Harold that he'd known us for three months and had a special interest in us.

After the show on the second night Harold came over to us and asked, "How are you doing on quitting smoking? I was talking to Mike earlier today, and he was extremely interested in how you two are doing."

"We're doing fine," I told him.

"I have a wonderful idea!" Harold said. "Why don't the two of you drop in some Saturday at Mike's church and surprise him?"

After all Mike had done for us we thought that would be the least we could do for him. It was a great idea, and we wondered why we hadn't thought of it before. "Could you give us the directions to his church?" I asked.

He gave us the directions and left the television studio for home.

The very next Saturday we got up, dressed, and left to attend Mike's church. As we walked into the church his wife, Dotty, was at the door; and as our eyes met, her mouth fell open and her eyes widened with surprise.

She hurried over to us. Her genuine warmth made us both feel good and really welcome.

"Please don't say anything to Mike about our being here because we want to surprise him," Alan suggested as we slipped into a back pew and very cautiously observed what was going on.

Alan and I, even though we didn't know much about them, had always thought of the Seventh-day Adventists as some strange cult. Although Mike, we thought, was different from what we'd expected. He must be an exception to the rest of them, we had decided.

We sat through the service wondering when all of the weird and strange stuff would begin. To our surprise it wasn't much different from any other Protestant service. And when the service ended we started toward the door to surprise Mike.

We slowly made our way closer to Mike, when all of a sudden he looked up and spotted us. I've never seen such a look of surprise before in my life.

He smiled from ear to ear, and he grabbed our hands and said, "I am so glad to see you. This is great! What a surprise! It's so nice to have you visit us!"

Chapter Three

The church was having a potluck dinner that day, and Mike insisted that we stay and eat with them. But Alan and I wanted to get home. After all, it was Saturday and we had work to do around the yard. Isn't that what most normal people do on Saturday? We had done what we had set out to do—give Mike a little surprise. Now we wanted out!

We didn't want to hurt Mike's feelings. After all, he was giving up one evening a week to give us Bible studies. We decided to stay and eat with them; then we could leave with a clear conscience.

Suddenly Alan and I looked at each other, and I'm sure he was thinking the same thing that I was thinking. "Yuk! Since they're Seventh-day Adventists, they're probably all vegetarians and only eat vegetables, nuts, and all that garbage!"

Just to be polite, we planned to put a little food on our plates and make it look good so we could eat and get out of there!

As we walked upstairs to the room where we were to eat, suddenly a woman jumped out in front of us, grabbed our hands, and said, "Hi, I know you, but you don't know me!"

I thought to myself, "Oh boy, a real weirdo."

She introduced herself as Doris, politely grabbed our arms, and directed us to a table saying, "You can eat here with me and my husband, Don."

"Oh, no! Will we ever be able to get out of here?" we thought.

This Doris told us how happy she was we had come to church that day. She said she knew a little about us through Mike, and had been watching us on the Five-Day plan on television. We learned that Doris and Don were not members of the church, but knew Mike and Dotty.

Mike and Dotty came over and talked to us for a while and again said, "We are so glad that the four of you are visiting us. Please feel free to come again."

We finally got out of there, but decided that other than it being so awkward because it was Saturday, being at that church hadn't been half bad. The service was similar to that which we were familiar with at our church, the Baptist Church, and the people seemed sincerely friendly.

The next Monday night at Bible study Mike again spoke of our visit and also mentioned that he'd watched us on television. "I really wanted you to know that I've been praying for the two of you for success and victory over your cigarette habit."

That week Doris and Don began coming to our Bible studies, and it was also the beginning of a wonderful friendship.

The neighbors in our block now started to wonder what was going on at our house. We were told by friends that they heard someone remark, "They've given up drinking, and now every week they have people going in and out of their house with Bibles in their hands! The next thing we'll find out is that they've gotten religious and have stopped smoking!"

Little did they know!

To hear people talking like that is exciting. It lets you know they are aware of and have noticed a change in your way of life.

After all, I surely felt different, and it was nice to know that it was noticeable! I was beginning to learn about Christ! It was extremely exciting, and I was now aware of so much more. I was starting to grow in Christ.

The next week Alan and I decided to attend Mike's church again. We wanted to see the look of pleased surprise on his face when he saw us. I wanted to go for yet another reason. I had just discovered that Alan had started to smoke again. He hadn't told me or anyone else because a lot of people at work thought that if Alan would quit smoking, I would too. He didn't want to disappoint those people, he told me later, so he was sneaking his cigarettes whenever he could.

It wasn't the fact that he was smoking again that bothered me so much as the fact that he didn't tell me. He had lied about it. All this I wanted to confide in Mike. I felt hurt and angry.

When I had the chance to talk to Mike alone I told him all about it.

Mike tried to calm me down by saying, "You've got to give him a chance."

"But if he's already lying to me about this, what else could he be lying about?"

When would I ever learn to really trust without creating more problems? I seemed always ready to blame someone else. I felt everyone was out to get me and hurt me. I couldn't see that others wanted a bit of love too.

I felt incapable of loving—of totally giving of myself. Why did I have such a hard time with this? Then the thought came to me, What special thing do You have in mind for me, Lord? What are You training me for by making me go through all this? I don't understand. Could it be that You want me to trust my husband and love him? Could it be You want me to develop a trust in You?

Mike asked if we would come over to the house and have dinner with him and Dotty that day. "Then I'll have a chance to talk to Alan," he added.

I accepted for both of us.

That Sabbath afternoon while Mike and Alan went for a walk, Dotty and I talked. But, as usual, I reacted like a selfish child. And when Alan and I returned home I decided that if Alan could smoke, I could too. I don't know what I was trying to prove, but I thought I could punish Alan or maybe I could make him feel guilty about his own smoking.

A few days later after we'd been to Mike's house I became ill. I had severe chest pain and decided not to go to work. The next day it was much worse. I started calling doctors until I found one who would see me.

The movement of the car made the pain worse, and by the time I got to the doctor's office I was in tears.

Immediately upon my arrival at the doctor's office they took me into the examining room.

They took X rays and then took blood to check my oxygen level because I was having such a hard time breathing.

The doctor ordered an injection for the pain after the blood had been drawn. "I'll be back as soon as I get the test results," he said. Then he added, "Try to rest the best you can so the injection can work."

When the doctor came back into the examining room

he said, "Your oxygen level is very low. There is a spot on your lung. I'm going to admit you into the hospital. We think you have a pulmonary embolism."

"Are you sure? I know I'm having a lot of pain, but that sounds so serious!" I told him.

"It could be pleurisy, but I'm not sure. We'll do some tests right away," he explained to me.

This scared me because my father had died of an embolism. I knew deep down that it probably didn't have any connection, but I decided not to let my mother or other relatives know I was in the hospital. I'd tell them about it when I got out. They would have worried so, and being three thousand miles away and not able to do anything would have made it worse.

After I was admitted they put me on oxygen, started an intravenous drip, and immediately brought me down to a special room to do a lung scan.

After the scan the doctor came into my room and said, "We're going to have to wait awhile for the result of the scan. It seems there was a spot that showed up, and a couple more doctors are being called in to help with the diagnosis. One doctor thinks it is pleurisy, but the other one believes it is an embolism. So they've called in a couple other doctors to help study the scan."

"Will I have to wait until morning to find out, or will you come back later and tell me?" I asked.

"As soon as they know for sure they're going to call me, and when I'm through with office hours I'll come by. So just hang in there for a while longer."

The doctor finally came back to the hospital early that evening and said, "The doctors finally agreed upon a diagnosis—an extreme case of pleurisy, which is a lot easier to deal with than the other possible diagnosis we had."

"That's for sure!" I agreed. "So what will be the next step? What is the treatment for pleurisy?" I asked.

"We'll keep you on oxygen and medication for the pain until you don't need it. We'll check your blood daily and also draw arterial blood to keep a close watch on your oxygen level until it improves. Other than that, there's not much else you can do."

I was so nervous and scared that I would take the oxygen tube out of my nose and go into the bathroom and smoke! I knew that of all times that I shouldn't be smoking it was now, but I started up again full force.

I remained on injections and pills for the pain until the doctor finally discharged me after eight days in the hospital. Before going home he gave me a prescription for the pain, which was still very bad.

I returned to the doctor's office week after week to have more arterial blood drawn to check on my oxygen level. It stayed low, and I remained on pain pills and felt extremely sick most of the time.

Doris became a very close friend at that time, visiting me every day, trying to cheer me up, and seeing to it that I was eating. She became a pillar of strength and a Christian example for me to follow. I will never forget her and will always maintain a special place in my heart for her.

Between Alice, Doris, and Dotty, Alan didn't have to worry about many meals. Mike also maintained regular visits while I was in the hospital and after I got out. He was quite worried that I was not recuperating as fast as I should. As a matter of fact, my test results still hadn't shown improvement at all since my discharge from the hospital. One day while Mike visited with me, he said, "I would like you to consider being anointed."

Of course, I had absolutely no idea at all what an

anointing was or what Mike was talking about. "What is an anointing?" I asked. "What do you do to me?"

"I don't really do anything except put oil on your head, have at least one elder present, and then have prayer," he explained.

Mike talked about it in great depth to me and suggested that I might think about it seriously since I'd been sick for such a long time.

Alan and I talked about it for a while and thought, "Why not! It certainly was worth a try!"

By that time I did believe, of course, that Jesus could heal me. Alan and I had had enough Bible studies to understand the things that Jesus could do if we only believed in Him.

I still felt very weak, but managed to get up and dressed that Sunday afternoon. Mike, the assistant pastor, an elder from the church, Alan, and our daughter Sondra kneeling around me formed a circle in the living room. We prepared for the anointing. It was brief and over soon. Everyone left but Mike, who stayed to talk to us for a while.

The next day I had a doctor's appointment, and Alan took me for the appointment. He wanted to talk to the doctor himself about my progress, he said.

After drawing blood for analysis the doctor examined me. By the time he had finished his examination, the blood-test results were back.

As you can guess, the test results were all perfectly normal. It was the first time in about a month and a half. I just praised the Lord. I was so elated that I could hardly wait to tell Mike the good news.

As soon as Alan dropped me off at home I started calling everywhere trying to locate Mike so I could tell him the test results.

Mike, of course, had already expressed his faith in

the outcome because of his relationship with the Lord.

Once I got back on my feet, our Monday-night Bible studies resumed. We naturally started getting more and more curious about this religion that meant so much to Mike and did so much for him.

Even when I talked to Alice, she never pushed her religion either; she just continued to love us through all our faults and to be our friend.

We started asking Mike some questions about why Seventh-day Adventists went to church on Saturdays. Of course, by this time we were actually observing the Sabbath from sunset to sunset ourselves and going to church every Saturday, even if we didn't fully understand why.

I guess it was the Lord's plan all along for us to find the truth, or else a year earlier when we were looking for someone to talk to, the Lord would have provided someone else for us, but He didn't!

We still, however, were having some difficulty in observing the Sabbath. It was very hard for us to get used to doing exactly opposite of what we were in the habit of doing. We had a struggle to get used to no television from sundown Friday to sundown Saturday. We had been big evening TV watchers.

Most Saturdays it wasn't too hard because we would be invited to people's home for dinner and to spend the afternoon. However, if we had to go directly home after church we would end up turning the television on. We found it very difficult breaking old habits, but have since learned to really enjoy the day.

It has also forced us to spend a whole day together doing things as a family unit, which we had never done before, for obvious reasons. We have grown to look forward to this time and to also enjoy each other's company.

At first, Sabbath keeping was a good excuse for not having to do any chores around the house, but we are slowly learning about the true meaning that the Sabbath should have. We have continued to let the Lord lead in our lives, even though sometimes I haven't been pleased with the direction He was leading.

It was during one of our usual Monday-night Bible studies when Mike announced, "My dream is about to come true. I am finally getting to go to Alaska." He had told us before that for more than twenty years he had wanted to go. "Now," he said, "I'm going to pastor a church in Anchorage."

When I first heard this I thought, "How can you do this to us, Mike?" I really thought he was deserting us in our hour of need. We were still learning, spiritually growing, and putting things back together.

We had grown to love him and to depend upon him to help us solve all our problems. We needed someone to talk to. Who else would understand our problems like Mike could? Who could we trust?

How could he do this to us? I thought over and over. I was resentful and felt extremely sorry for myself.

At that time I didn't realize that this was the best thing that could have happened to us and to other people in the church who had grown dependent on Mike.

I felt rejected and frightened about the future. My faith waivered. We were looking too much to the person, Mike, for answers, instead of to the Lord.

Alan and I, once we found out Mike's plans, had talked quite extensively about what we were going to do now that Mike was leaving.

The next Sabbath Mike gave his farewell sermon, and there weren't many dry eyes in the whole church. He was respected, depended on, and loved by everyone there. How we all hated to see him go.

That night there was to be a special vesper service for Mike and his family members at the church. Of course, we planned to attend.

Many gave short testimonies as to what a change knowing Mike had made in their lives and how he had led them to the Lord.

At last Alan and I got up to pay our tribute to Mike. We publicly announced our intentions to become baptized into the church.

Many people who had become good friends of ours were thrilled about the news and for us.

Since Mike would now be away from his Oregon church for a while and only home on weekends, we decided that we would wait for baptism until one of the weekends Mike was home. "We want you to be the one to baptize us because you were the one that led us to the Lord and have helped us so much in the last year," I told Mike.

"I would be hurt if anyone else did baptize you both," he said with his usual smile. "I'd even come down from Alaska for the occasion. I would be honored and pleased to baptize you both," he said.

Many gave thanks that evening for all Mike's help, love, and guidance. Finally good-byes had to be said.

We continued our Monday-night Bible studies without Mike. It had seemed that Mike always knew if I didn't understand something or if I had a question—which was almost always. I guess he could tell by the expression on my face! But now he was gone. Alan and I really did enjoy and look forward to the studies, though, because they got us through the rest of the week. We also liked them because we knew it was in preparation for our baptism. I was on a real high for a long time, I was so looking forward to *that* day.

Before I found Christ I was nervous and thought I really needed my cigarettes! I had given up drinking and felt, I guess, that I needed something to help my nerves—especially when I was upset with my husband, the children, or the day itself was a bummer!

But neither Alan or I were ready to give up smoking or to make that total commitment to the Lord.

For months I talked about quitting, going as far as to pray to the Lord at night saying, "OK, Lord, tomorrow's the day. I'll be calling on You a lot."

But the next morning would come, and I would light up immediately. I was being convicted by the Lord to stop smoking, but I was not willing to cooperate with Him. I was, at this point, still fighting the Lord not wanting to really give in all the way. I wanted happiness in my home; I wanted security and love; above all, I wanted peace. I guess what I really wanted were the fruits of the Spirit as listed in Galatians 5:22, 23. I knew the only way I was going to get this was to make a total commitment of myself to the Lord.

It was two weeks before we were to be baptized on February 24, 1979. Mike had come home for the weekend, and he naturally came to see us. We had a long talk that lasted two and a half hours, discussing some self problems that Alan and I were still having. At the end of the conversation, as Mike was getting ready to leave, he asked, "How are you two doing with your smoking?"

Alan answered, "To be honest, not too good, Mike. We're both struggling."

"Yes," I spoke up, "I'm sorry to admit it, but I'm still smoking; it's so hard to give it up."

"As you know I also smoked once. Until you are

ready to give it totally to the Lord you will not be able to give it up,'' Mike told us.

''I know that, Mike. I have been having such a battle trying to make that commitment to the Lord. I do so desperately want to stop smoking,'' I said.

''If you want to postpone the baptism for a while, I could come down from Alaska to baptize you whenever you want,'' he said.

Alan and I looked at each other, then Alan said, ''No, we don't want to postpone the baptism for anything. We have been preparing for it for a long time now and are looking forward to it. We want to go ahead as planned to be baptized in two weeks.''

''In that case, before I can baptize you, because of the beliefs of the church, you should have at least two weeks of not smoking under your belts. You really should have more, but since I know you and your intentions, I can vouch for you,'' he told us.

I thought to myself, ''He surely isn't giving us much time or notice. Our baptism is just two weeks away. That means that I will have to stop smoking right now! Tonight!''

Chapter Four

I thought, "I can't do it; not that fast!" Of course, with that statement I put myself in a negative state of mind. I started right away with a case of the "guilties" because I did continue to smoke for a few days!

I knew I wanted to be baptized and to do everything right, but there was this something that held me back from trusting and relying on God for strength. After Mike left that evening, Satan really started working on me. I had a real battle with myself, the Lord, and Satan; and I tried to fight the battle all alone.

Even after Alan and I had gone to bed, I struggled on alone. The water bed felt hard and uncomfortable. Darkness was not only around me but within me. Alan slept peacefully beside me, while I felt completely alone. Something dreadful seemed to be closing in on me.

As I struggled in my mind I decided to go up into the loft, where there were four skylight windows. There I would pray!

I had never done this before, and the only reason I can think of was that I thought that I would feel closer to God by looking up into the heavens while I prayed.

Now, being a very new Christian and not realizing what I was doing, I made a great mistake. I thought in my mind, "OK, Satan, I will give you one more chance to get me and that's it." I said this right out loud. And that was all Satan needed to hear. He made his move quickly. The more I planned my strategy in my mind, the more frightened I became, until I was trembling. I suddenly realized that I could never go up into the loft, because in my state of mind I knew the devil was waiting for me, and he would get me. I was overcome by fright.

Then it happened! He appeared to me! I will never forget it for as long as I live! It was in a dark cloud that I saw that awful face with a terrifying grin. His diamond-shaped red eyes piercingly looked down at me.

"I have you where I want you now; all you have to do is come up into the loft!" he sneeringly said.

I became hysterical and started praying while crying, "In the name of Jesus leave me alone! In the name of Jesus I demand you to go away!" Then I cried out, "Please, Lord, help me! I'm so frightened. I can't remember how to pray; please, make him go away," I begged.

I was sitting up in the bed, crying, rocking back and forth and praying, and Alan woke up.

"What is the problem? Why are you crying? What is going on?" he asked.

At that moment I couldn't answer. All I could do was rock and cry. Finally Alan got me to lie down. I curled up into a fetal position and kept crying. I felt as if something was pulling me in two different directions.

"I feel like I might leave; the devil is pulling me. My body feels like it's in a tug-of-war, the devil pulling me in one direction and the Lord pulling in the other," I at last cried out.

At long last I stopped crying enough to tell Alan what had happened. He kept questioning me. He wasn't sure that this thing had really happened. Was it all my imagination? But at last he realized it was a very real thing to me.

I wanted to call Mike and have him pray for me, but I knew he had been with us late enough and he needed his sleep. You see, it was now around 3 o'clock in the morning and Mike had to leave that day for California. We didn't call him.

Alan opened the Bible and read the first and second epistles of Peter to me. By the time he had finished it was almost 4:30 in the morning, and I fell asleep, exhausted.

I woke the next day around noon, still extremely tired. I called Mike, but he had already left his house. I then called Doris, but she wasn't home either. I just stayed in bed, afraid to go out of my bedroom. I would hear footsteps, noises, and accuse Alan of making them, but he was sitting at the table working on an airplane model and said, "I don't hear any noises or anything."

Later that day I did get through to Mike—just as he was to leave for the airport. I told him of my experience, and he assured me that he'd be praying for me and he'd write that night when he got to California. Then he gave me some Bible promises to look up.

The next evening being Monday, we had our usual Bible study. How I looked forward to it, knowing I really needed it.

I sat down in my usual spot in the living room and then realized I could see up into the loft a little. This scared me, and I moved to another seat. Meanwhile, I kept thinking about what Mike had said about smoking and our baptism. I just had to give up smoking. It wouldn't be two weeks of abstinence if I stopped now, but maybe he'd baptize us anyway.

I was starting to feel pressured because of the baptism, but couldn't bear the disappointment if we had to postpone it. I had been looking forward to it for too long a time, and no one was going to take that away from me! Then I started to reason with myself. "*Now* isn't the time to quit with all that I'm going through with the devil bearing down on me so much."

But that Tuesday night I decided that I was *going* to quit and on my own too! I really did want to stop, but Satan started using the pressure that I was feeling to his advantage.

I had been trying to stick pretty much to the diet of the Five-Day Plan. I seemed to be praying all the time—not really wanting to!

On Wednesday morning I got up and went to Doris's house because I didn't have to work, and didn't want to be alone in the house all morning. Around noon we came back to my house for our usual Wednesday-afternoon prayer group there. We ended that day by going up into the loft to pray, and we demanded that the devil leave this house.

In prayer, we claimed Bible promises, especially Matthew 18:19, 20, which reads basically that where two or more are gathered together asking anything in His name, it will be granted. We also asked that the Lord give me strength to meet the challenge to quit smoking!

The following four days were awful. I became more irritable by the day and started to blame others for the hard time I was having.

Mike had written a letter from California with some encouraging words and Bible promises. But Satan saw to it that I didn't receive that letter until the next week, after the crisis was over.

By Sabbath of that week, which was only three days

later, I was "climbing the walls," as the expression goes. The devil certainly worked overtime on me that day.

I wanted no part of Sabbath School, church, or anyone. All during Sabbath School class I sat rigidly in the pew holding my head down, refusing to listen or take part in any way. My resentment kept building. By the time the church worship hour started I was ready to punch anyone that looked at me. I even got up during the sermon and planned to go into the ladies' room and put my fists through the mirrors. But on the way I ran into a friend who was in my prayer group and who knew what I was going through. So she talked to me until the end of church. Actually I let out my hostilities on her.

Thank the Lord she understood what was happening. She had gone through such an experience about seven months before. But at this point, I felt that I was fighting a losing battle.

After church Doris's daughter, Shelley, who was to be baptized with Alan and me, came up to me with a big smile. "I'm so excited about being baptized next week. Aren't you?" she asked.

I snapped back, "I don't think I really want to be baptized after all, if I have to go through all this!"

Shelley, with a hurt and confused expression on her face, slowly moved away from me not saying anything else. Alan looked at me with a queer expression on his face, and I'm sure extremely embarrassed by my actions, took me by the arm and said, "Let's go home."

By the time we were almost home I finally said, "Give me a cigarette! I can't stand it anymore." I was so hostile and bitter. Alan himself was still smoking, and I didn't feel that that was fair at all.

Alan handed me a cigarette and the lighter but refused to light it for me. "I respect you for giving it up, and I won't help you to smoke by lighting it for you," he said.

The rest of that Sabbath was like a nightmare. I was so rebellious and bitter toward anyone who tried to talk to me. I smoked four or five cigarettes that Sabbath afternoon.

That was March 3, 1979, exactly one week before our baptism, and it was also my last day of smoking! I praise God for that!

I started with a case of the "guilties" and tried to rationalize my feelings about smoking, because it had been a cherished sin of mine. "After all," I thought, "there were other people in the church that smoked or drank! Why should I have to give it up?"

As the day went on I had a few more cigarettes. We didn't have any plans for this Sabbath. We were alone. We ended up turning on the television set, and that made me feel guilty too!

Later that evening I called a friend that I had been quite rude to that morning and apologized. During our conversation I realized that I couldn't go on this way. I *had* to make a commitment one way or the other.

You see, I had never truly loved, trusted, or totally committed myself to anyone—not even my husband. This was very hard for me to do. I think it was the hardest thing I've ever done in my life.

The reason I was so hostile was not because I had been told if I wanted to be baptized I had to give up smoking. But because I finally had to decide whether I would let the devil rule me, my thoughts, and actions, or whether I would let the Lord have my life.

I knew I didn't want to do my own thing and follow my own instincts, which were of the devil; so the only way to go was with God!

I had never given up myself to the Lord completely, and that was what I was struggling with now. I was clinging to that last vice, wanting to do right, because I was being convicted to do it, but subconsciously I was fighting the Lord.

The next day Alice came over, and I was laying it on her also. She fortunately realized the battle I was going through. About a half hour after Alice left, Mike called from California. "In the last hour I've been thinking about you and was impressed to call you," he said.

"I was just talking about you to Alice, telling her how much I needed to talk to you," I replied. I felt relieved when I heard his voice, and knew that the Lord had His hand in this.

"Have you gotten my letters?" he asked. "How are you doing?"

"I haven't received anything except a postcard with some Bible promises on it," I told him.

"The devil really has been harassing you this last week, hasn't he?" Mike remarked. "I have been worried about Alan and you because of what I said about smoking." He paused.

"Yes, it has been a real struggle this last week, but I'm hanging in there," I assured him.

"I'm glad to hear that," Mike said. "I will make an exception in Alan's and your case about the two weeks, as long as you are trying and really feel you have a victory over this habit."

"Hearing that makes me feel a whole lot better, and I'm sure it will make Alan feel better too. It relieves a lot of pressure. I still feel I have to tell you how I've been feeling and the resentments that have built up."

"I'm sure there are a lot, Sharon," Mike said. "Remember I went through what you are going through myself a few years back. Go ahead.''

I started out in full force and told him my previous thoughts: ''I know of other people in the church that smoke and drink. Why do I have to give it up? Who do these people in the Seventh-day Adventist Church think they are to judge me?''

I continued telling how I felt: ''What makes them feel they are any better than I am? I have to report only to God, not to them! Who do you think you are, Mike, telling me I can't be baptized unless I give up smoking? Are you saying I'm not good enough to be baptized?''

Mike interrupted my harangue. ''Your mind sure has been working overtime, hasn't it? It's better that you get it all out; it will make you feel better,'' he said.

''I thought baptism was supposed to be the start of a new you, where the old one died and the new one grew in the Lord,'' I said.

''That's true, Sharon.'' Mike answered quickly. ''Of course, I hope you realize and understand the doctrines and beliefs of the church. No one is judging you! The devil knows he's losing two more people to the Lord, so he's giving it everything he's got, one last time,'' Mike explained.

''Well,'' I went on, ''I've been thinking, what's the use? I just won't be baptized; I'll join another church if that's the way you feel! But every Sunday that I went to another church I would feel as if I were committing a sin! I'm already convicted that Saturday is the true Sabbath day.''

At this point Mike spoke up and said, ''Praise the Lord for that.''

Mike, I am sure, knew my feelings and the pain I was going through right then, and he could sympathize with me.

I knew what was right. I was rebelling against the

Lord. I knew smoking wasn't good for me, and I really did want to give it up; but this is when I realized for the first time that I had never totally committed my life to Christ, not really.

I knew Mike's story and his battle with cigarettes. I figured that if he could do it, so could I!

We talked on the phone a few minutes longer, even though he was calling from California.

"I'm proud of you and how well you're doing, considering what you've been going through," he said. "Keep up the good work and remember I'll be praying for you." With that we said our good-byes and hung up.

I started that day, for the first time, kneeling when I prayed. I would claim Bible promises and thank God, for I knew that He would take this burden from me. I prayed and prayed—to the point that I could feel His arms around me. Tears of love came running down my cheeks. It was at this point that I completely committed my life and my problems to God and started my positive thinking.

If God can remove the desire to smoke from Mike, He can do it for me! Mike's no better a person than I am—so therefore God will help me too! I said.

I told God in several of our conversations, "If I have to battle with the desire to smoke for six months to a year in my human form, I would just give in to it." I knew I would! "But You can make me stronger for other trials and things I'll have to go through by removing the desire to smoke completely from me," I prayed.

At this point I started my game plan. It was exactly a week before our baptism, and I made that the Lord's and my victory day.

I was using the symbolism of baptism for the end of

the habit. I decided, with the help of God, that when I went under the water that that would be the death of my desire and of the old self. When I came up out of the water, it would be the birth of a new person!

I then started to pray like I never have before—really meaning it and submitting myself to the Lord.

You see, I believed that the Lord would do this for me. When praying, I asked God, believed He would do it, and thanked Him for doing it right then and there. I did this each time I prayed.

I also, once I'd learned the problem, turned my back on it and kept my eyes fixed on the solution—Jesus!

Remember, through Jesus anything is possible. I think the great victory the Lord gave me over cigarettes is the result of many things: I had to believe first He could remove any desire—any desire I had to smoke. I claimed Bible promises every day, depending on which ones moved me that day. I asked the Lord for help—sometimes I begged for it. I thanked Him for answering my prayers. Every time before I prayed I would try to relax, get comfortable, take deep breaths, and do anything that would get me in the right frame of mind. I never dwelt on the problem. I kept myself busy, and every time I would feel my subconscious mind wandering back onto the problem I would get up, move, go to another room, do something different—anything to change my train of thought. This is also when I would get down on my knees and do a lot of praying.

I read and reread "Solution-Centered Praying" from Glenn Coon's book *The Science of Prayer–Its ABC's*. It helped me through a lot of tough times. I would wholeheartedly recommend the book to anyone.

Do you know that before long I really started believing, and the more I believed the better I felt and the easier it became to pray. Don't get me wrong. In that last week there were a couple of hard times. I even called Mike long distance in California for some moral support one day.

But it was a lot easier once I decided to let God help and to make that final commitment to trust someone that much—especially someone you can't see! What a neat thing to realize and do!

I know you or anyone can also have this victory if you just give the problem to the Lord and truly believe He can help you.

Remember, I prayed for a couple of months before I really wanted any help. So I know you can be free too if you will only ask, believe, and claim!

I feel confident in saying that I know that if you have a problem like mine and put it in God's hands, you will have a victory like mine! I also praise God for the opportunity to once again give my testimony, which is a great thrill for me!

Alan at this time was still struggling with his smoking, but he kept trying to quit.

It was warm and sunny, the day victory for me finally came. I talked to Dotty and Doris that day, "I have victory over cigarettes," I exclaimed. "The Lord has completely taken the desire away, just as I claimed He would." I felt as if I were riding on a cloud. I had never before felt so elated.

On the evening before the day of baptism, two of our new friends, John and Marsha Raugh, came over to go over the doctrinal beliefs of the church and to make sure we truly understood all these things.

That last week we had talked several times with the Raughs and had even joked occasionally, "I suppose at the last minute you'll be telling us that we can no longer wear orange shirts on Tuesday."

Of course this was only a joke, but we were still a little worried that just before we would be baptized that someone would remember something that hadn't been mentioned before. We really would have been surprised if nothing had been forgotten.

But something had been forgotten. It pertained to jewelry.

"Seventh-day Adventists don't wear jewelry," John told us that Friday night.

"What?" I exclaimed. I had pierced ears. I had several pair of beautiful earrings. I had three or four very expensive necklaces. I had two crosses with diamonds and the gold bar that Alan had brought me after one of his trips.

"Well, now you tell us. This is something else," I said. I twisted the wedding band I wore on my left hand. "I couldn't take that off. It lets everyone know that I am committed to someone. By wearing that ring I was saved a lot of explanations," I reasoned. "Taking it off would hurt Alan too."

John and Marsha Raugh felt extremely bad that the wearing of jewelry had never come up before. John kept apologizing over and over. He just assumed that it had been discussed.

"I hope there isn't anything else they've forgotten to tell us," I said.

For some time there was a silence in the room. Then I spoke up. "I have committed myself to the Lord. I have changed my life so much. What's the big deal about giving up the wearing of jewelry?"

It was sometime later when talking to Dotty Jones that I learned the reason why Seventh-day Adventists don't wear jewelry, and it has all made sense to me.

Dotty said, "Seventh-day Adventists don't wear jewelry because it draws false attention to the person.

When we look at a person we should be attracted to them because of the Christlike image we see."

That makes sense to me. I don't want anything to stand in the way of the Christlike image that I want people to see.

Now, going back to my day of baptism. The Lord gave me total victory over my cigarette habit. I had no desire whatsoever to smoke. From that day on, the very smell of cigarette smoke in a room or on someone's breath turns my stomach. I never had realized how terrible it was for friends coming over to our house to smell cigarette smoke all around them when they themselves didn't smoke. I praise God for giving me the victory.

I wonder now at all the money we spent on lifesavers and other mints to put in our mouths before we went to church to hide the fact that we were still smoking. I wonder also how we got along spending so much money on cigarettes.

With what anticipation Alan and I went to church the day of our baptism! Mike Jones and all the other church members greeted us warmly.

The moment arrived.

I asked if Mike would share with the congregation before our baptism how grateful I am to the Lord for my healing after anointing when I was so extremely ill. I also wanted the congregation to know of the tremendous victory the Lord had given me over the cigarette habit. "Can you do that?" I asked.

"That's a wonderful idea," Mike agreed.

Alan and I walked down into the baptismal font. We were the last two to be baptized that day. Alan went first. I followed him.

The great moment had arrived, and Mike was saying those beautiful words, "I baptize you in the name of the Father, and of the Son, and of the Holy Ghost. Amen.'' Mike lowered me into the water. I was praying all the while. When I came up out of the water there seemed to be a light all around. I heard music. What a feeling! I was high—on a natural high with the Lord!

I had never felt that way before—even after a few drinks. If this is an example of what was going to be happening in my life, I loved it! I couldn't wait to see what would happen next. That really was the start of many wonderful things that would be happening in my life.

The Lord has blessed me with many opportunities to witness to people about the victory over smoking I have and how I did it. It has encouraged many people to claim Bible promises in areas in which they needed help.

It makes me feel good inside to be helping people. It also makes me more thankful to the Lord for what He has done for me.

I am now more comfortable talking about God to other people, which I had never been able to do before. It seems as though He has gifted me since my baptism.

Some people recently have come to me for advice and help, which also tends to build my faith. It is a terrific feeling to be able to help other people for a change instead of being the one who needs the help. And from the bottom of my heart I say, ''Thank You, Lord!''

Chapter Five

The days passed all too quickly. The day of our baptism came and ended all too soon. Mike left shortly after for Alaska. It was time to start making it on our own with only the Lord leading us.

We had turned our lives and priorities around and decided that we would try to sell the house. Alan and I were wanting to send the children to our church school. We also wanted to pay a faithful tithe, and we needed to get out of debt.

Dotty, Mike's wife, stayed in town until her children were out of school that year and their house sold, before she joined Mike in Alaska. So we women friends continued in our Wednesday-afternoon prayer group, Dotty and I both claiming Bible promises for the Lord to sell our homes.

One day at work one of the girls told me that there was a long-distance phone call for me. I couldn't figure out who would be calling me at work, let alone long distance. I never stopped to think that it might be Mike.

I got on the phone and was totally surprised to hear Mike's voice; he was calling me from Alaska. I couldn't imagine what would be so important that he would call me at home first and then at work, and long distance at that! What could the reason be?

"Are you still interested in spreading God's word and helping people?" he asked.

"Of course I am," I told him. "Why?"

"There are a couple of women up here who are having a problem with smoking. Would you please write them a letter or testimony of your victory over smoking?" he asked.

Here was something I could do not only for my Saviour, but to show a little of my appreciation to Mike for his help.

"Yes, Mike, I'd be honored to do that for you and for my Saviour."

He explained what he wanted and we hung up.

Once confronted with having to write to two women that I had never met, I thought, "I will never be able to do this." I had no idea what they were like. For once in my life I didn't know what to say.

That was unusual for me because all through my life my nickname had been Motor-Mouth! And now I was upset because I thought I would lose my chance to help someone because I couldn't think of anything to say.

I prayed to the Lord to please give me the wisdom and knowledge to be able to write an inspirational testimony to these two women.

As always I have to praise God for being with me and giving me such a victory. It took me a whole week to finally get the letter written. When I finished it, Dotty typed it for me—a three-page, single-spaced letter.

I was nervous about sending that letter to two people I didn't know. I even called Mike one night in Alaska, I was so unsure of myself. He reassured me that it was a beautiful letter.

Dotty had also told me the letter was definitely inspired by the Lord.

I have since given a copy of that letter to a lot of people here where I live, and I hope the Lord will soften the hearts that read it.

We continued our Wednesday prayer group, claiming Bible promises and getting answers to our prayers. It was wonderful the way the Lord worked in all our lives.

One Sunday morning I was asked to go to work that afternoon. Our realtor was planning on having an open house, and we had plans for the afternoon but changed our minds once I found out I had to work. We spent the morning doing some yard work during the open house. A couple with four children came to see the place. They stayed a long time and seemed to be interested in what they saw.

They were still there when it was time for me to leave for work. I thought I heard them mentioning something about making an offer. I didn't want to leave not knowing, but I had to go.

All the way to work I kept thinking, "O Lord, I know this is it. Please, let these people buy our house."

Around 10:30 that night Alan and our realtor came to the hospital where I was working to get my signature on some papers. The couple had made an offer, but we made a counteroffer.

The next night we were having our usual Bible study. We were almost finished when our realtor arrived at the front door. "I have just put the 'Sold' sign on the 'For Sale' sign out front."

"That's great! I'm so glad. I can scarcely believe it. Thank you," I told the realtor.

The couple had bought the house, and I praised

God and thanked Him. We closed the Bible study after the realtor left with prayers of thanks for another answer to prayer. The Lord seemed to be continually blessing us with answers to our prayer requests.

We were so elated that we started selling our furniture in preparation to moving into a smaller home. We would no sooner put an ad in the paper than whatever we were selling was sold. Everything just seemed to be going our way for a change, we thought!

Our house hadn't been sold for more than a month when we got loan approval for our new house. We heard everything was going fine with the loan for the people who were planning on buying our house.

I couldn't understand what was taking so long with their loan when our realtor told us, "Well, you know you folk agreed they could assume your mortgage instead of taking out a new loan of their own with the interest rates being so high."

"Is that what's taking so long? I didn't realize that it took any longer to get loan approval if taking over an existing mortgage," I said.

"Yes, it does. So be patient. Everything is going along on schedule," he told me.

Soon after this at our usual Wednesday prayer group we decided to write down the answers to our prayers and the dates when our prayers were answered. Suddenly Dotty and I realized that we had listed and sold our homes within a week of each other. We had prayed about selling our homes, and it had happened almost miraculously. Soon she would be able to join Mike in Alaska, and Alan and I would be out of debt.

It wasn't long after the house sold that Mike flew down from Alaska to pack up their household goods and take his family with him to Alaska. Fortunately, we managed to see him a few times before they left for good. We had grown to depend on and look to Mike for help and courage—now we would have to trust entirely on God, we knew.

It seemed that everything Mike did or said was because he was abundantly blessed by the Lord. He was God's servant, and he did his serving extremely well. Now we had to learn to look to the Lord for our answers instead of to the man, Mike.

Just before time to move from our big house to the smaller one, I got sick and had to have some lab work done at the hospital. The liver-function tests were not good. It was decided that the tests should be done again in a couple of days.

When the tests were completed by the lab technician at the hospital where I worked, he recommended that I see a doctor at once.

I called my friend Alice Rogers, who worked in medical records, and asked, "Do you know a good doctor I could see? All I have is a general practitioner. I like him and have nothing against him, but I'd like an Adventist doctor that comes to this hospital."

"I think you'd like Dr. Muderspach," Alice said. "Why don't I call him for you since I know him. I can probably get you in faster. OK?"

"Thanks, Alice," I said. "I'll wait to hear from you as to when he can see me."

She called me back quite quickly. "I've made an appointment for you at nine o'clock tomorrow morning."

Sitting in the waiting room the next morning I began to get nervous as I always do when I go to a doctor. But when I finally got into the examining room and the doctor came in, he put me at ease immediately. "Hello, Sharon," he said in a warm friendly way. "I'm Dr. Muderspach."

We talked for a while; I gave him the results of the tests that had been done. He examined me. "It could be so many things. Even appendicitis," he said. "If you're not any better by Monday, or if you get worse, call me."

He gave me a prescription for pain and his home phone number because he wasn't on call that weekend but wanted me to call him anyway. I thanked him and left.

Later that afternoon the pain was worse, and even though I hated to bother the doctor again, I called him.

"I think you should go to the hospital," he said. "I'll call and make arrangements to get you admitted, and meet you there."

"I'll be there in about forty-five minutes," I told him as I hung up.

When I got to the hospital, got through with the admitting procedure, and got up to my room Dr. Muderspach was there waiting for me.

While he began examining me and asking questions about my past and about my work in the hospital, I began to relax and gain more confidence in him.

I told him I'd only been working at the hospital a few months. I told him I was actually a medical assistant but hadn't been able to find a part-time job in a doctor's office.

The doctor exclaimed, "Oh really? It just so happens that the woman that works for me is pregnant and will be leaving in a couple of months. I could use someone else now, because she's trying to run the whole office by herself, and there's too much work for one person. So I will need two full-time office helpers."

"I've worked full time before." I sighed. "I'm really only interested in part-time work now. It's too bad too because the job sounds ideal," I told him.

"If you change your mind, keep me in mind and I'll give you an interview," he said. He finished his examination, made sure I had all the proper medications ordered for the weekend, and left.

They had me on intravenous feedings and Demerol injections for the pain, but still didn't know what was causing my problem.

A few days after I had been admitted to the hospital, Alan came in with bad news. "The people who were going to buy our house just backed out of the deal!" he said.

"You're kidding! How can they just back out like that? What are we going to do?" I questioned.

"Don't worry, things will work out for the best; they always do!" he told me, trying to calm my fears.

We had already sold a sofa, chair, china cabinet, and dinette set in preparation of our move into a smaller house.

My first thought was, How could the Lord allow this to happen to us? What are we going to do now? I became quite depressed, with feelings of resentment toward God and most of all self-pity for myself! "I am doomed to never be happy or out of debt!" I thought, wallowing in self-pity.

During this ordeal Dr. Muderspach was so patient and understanding, a true Christian. This was so new to me, to meet a doctor who wasn't a physician just for the recognition and the money he got out of it. No, Dr. Muderspach was different, a Christian, and a doctor because he truly cared about people and wanted to help them.

On his morning rounds he would come into my room and find me upset. He'd come over to the bed and talk to me, drawing out the things that were troubling me. I would open up and feel free to tell him everything that had happened to Alan and me regarding our struggles before baptism. I told him that now we wanted to do everything right, and how the sale of our house had fallen through. "Why! Oh why!" I would cry.

"It's hard to understand why some things happen," he'd tell me, "but there is always a reason, Sharon. God knows the end from the beginning."

"Yes, I've been told that." I'd sniffle. "But we're trying so hard to get out of debt and do things right. I just don't understand why the Lord won't allow us to sell the house."

Dr. Muderspach would sympathize, "I can't answer that. We don't always understand why things happen, but I do know that the Lord is always with us. I know it doesn't seem that way sometimes, but we have to be patient. There is a reason for everything, and I'm sure there's one for what has happened."

"I just wish I knew why. It seems like the harder we try to change, the more barriers we keep running into," I told him over and over.

But Dr. Muderspach always answered, "Maybe things are going too fast and you have to slow down a little. Just trust the Lord, Sharon."

"It's easy for you to say," I'd lash out. "What trial have you had? You've been an Adventist all your life; you're a doctor; you don't have financial problems."

"I know it seems that way and maybe I haven't had as many problems as you have had, Sharon, but you have to learn to trust the Lord!"

I didn't learn for at least another year to fully trust. I wondered why all Dr. Muderspach could say to me as I lay in that bed worrying was, "Just trust the Lord, Sharon; just trust the Lord!" I felt envious of his faith and trust in the Lord and wondered if I would ever get to that point in my life.

After I had been in the hospital almost two weeks Dr. Muderspach called in another doctor, a surgeon, to see if he could find out what was wrong with me. He decided to do an exploratory operation. They scheduled the surgery for the next day.

During the surgery the doctors found an ovarian cyst and some adhesions. "These things could have been the cause of your pain," the doctor said after the surgery. And a few days later I was released from the hospital.

I had learned that being a Christian wasn't easy and once you accept Christ everything isn't a bed of roses. The Christian has to make a daily commitment. One needs to ask the Lord to come into one's life daily to guide and direct. It is so much harder to be good, especially if you think someone isn't nice to you. It's not in our human nature to be good. We have to pray continually for help.

I got even more depressed after coming home from the hospital. I stopped praying and thought terrible thoughts about the Lord.

"It just isn't worthwhile being a Christian if I have to constantly struggle!" I decided.

Chapter Six

A week after I got out of the hospital, which was June 23, 1979, our two children were baptized. They had been studying with the pastor for quite a few weeks in preparation for this day.

What a beautiful day that Sabbath was. Alan supplied the special music that day. It was my first day out of bed since my discharge from the hospital. I cried, not from sorrow but from sheer joy. I praised the Lord that my children had decided to join God's people. I was proud that the children had made their own decision to be baptized and followed it through, although they were only nine and ten and a half, and *that*, we felt, was a little young. But we had decided that if we said No, that we might be turning their desire off. We didn't want that. We'd had enough of that in our household to last a lifetime.

Our oldest child, Sondra, was now getting ready for her first trip to camp. I had wanted to send both of them to camp for the week, but later realized we didn't have the money because the sale of our house fell through. I had been planning on that sale to help us with a lot of things!

When I was in the hospital, some friends had decided to pay the expenses for our children to go to camp. But when we later found out there was room for only one of the children, I chose Sondra because she was the older of the two.

As my health improved my faith began now to develop once more. The Lord was providing for us in different ways than we had planned or even wanted, but He was providing.

I couldn't believe that friends that I didn't know very well were willing to help us by sending our children to camp, and to do that just out of love for another Christian. They weren't even doing it expecting something in return.

How grateful I am for friends like that!

I will never forget all the many people who put up with me when I was at my worst and continued to show me Christ's love even when I didn't want to see it!

We are all now baptized in the Seventh-day Adventist Church and will continue our growth in Christ together as a family unit. We are now one totally united family, all working for the same purpose—to hasten the return of our Lord and Saviour, Jesus Christ.

Alan and I started to do some serious talking about what we were going to do regarding our financial situation. We decided we would have to make the best of things, going on until the Lord decided to change our situation. We decided I would go back to work full time to help out. Immediately I talked to my boss at the hospital about working full time.

"Yes, we can use the help, but of course you realize you'll have to work every other weekend," he said.

This didn't excite me too much because it would have been enough of an adjustment for everyone in the family with me going back to work full time, but to have to work weekends too was unthinkable. Then I remembered my discussion with Dr. Muderspach the day he had admitted me to the hospital. Since I was scheduled to have a checkup with him in a couple of days, I decided to ask him if he had hired anyone yet for the job in his office.

"No, I haven't filled it yet," Dr. Muderspach told me when I asked about the job. "Why don't you talk to my assistant out front and set up a time to come in for an interview."

A few days later I had an interview and left the office feeling very positive and excited about working for an Adventist doctor. The hours would be great too! Monday, Wednesday, and Thursday were full working days with two-hour lunch break on Wednesday. Tuesday and Friday were half days, and we never had to work on the weekends. Even though it would be a full-time job I would still have two afternoons a week off.

I called a few days later to discover I had the job and they wanted me to begin the next week. This, I felt sure, was an answer to prayer.

It was quite an adjustment working full time again, but it was also extremely challenging. Dr. Muderspach, a patient and easy man to work for, was appreciative of everything I did for him. At the end of every day he thanked me, and if I had to stay a little late he would apologize for keeping me late. "He's the kind of boss everyone always dreams of having," I said over and over. Between him and the patients it was the best job I'd ever had. I actually looked forward to going to work every day.

I hadn't been working there long when I met his wife, Elaine, a sweet, beautiful person herself. The Muderspachs were an example of what a Christian

Adventist family should be.

One Sabbath Dr. Muderspah asked if Alan would play the trumpet for his Sabbath School program, and later for the church service. He also invited us to his home for Sabbath dinner. My mother, visiting with us at the time, came with us.

Alan had just gotten over a bad chest cold and was worried that he wouldn't be able to play to the best of his capabilities, but he did fine considering how he felt. After church we followed the doctor to his house in our car and had a delicious meal at the Muderspach home. Elaine, a gracious hostess, helped to make a memorable day for us. On the way home my mom remarked about how nice the Muderspachs were.

"I can't believe it!" she said. "Imagine a doctor inviting you to his home. The doctor is so down-to-earth—just an ordinary person. Most doctors are so high and mighty, but he makes you feel so relaxed and comfortable. If I had a boss and job with working conditions like that, Sharon, I would never leave. It's too good to be true!"

I laughed. "Don't you think I know that! I have no intentions of ever quitting; besides with all the bills we have now it will take at least five years to get them all paid off. Being a Christian makes the Muderspachs different and wonderful," I told her.

Not long after this, my friend Doris got a part-time job. The afternoon I had off she had to work.

"I'm starting to feel a separation from my Christian friends," I told Doris one day.

"I know what you mean," she answered. "Now that I'm working I find it hard to organize my time."

"I know," I agreed. "I too am having a problem. As much as I love my job, I'm having a time putting my priorities in order. I am troubled too because I don't see much of my friends anymore.''

"Just give me a little time to get organized with this new job, and maybe we can work something out," Doris said.

"I'm having a hard time understanding what has been happening to me. First the Joneses leave, our Monday-night Bible study ends, I start working, you start working, our Wednesday-afternoon study ends, and I'm seeing less and less of my Christian friends. I desperately miss that fellowship; it's what keeps me going. With all that and the house still not selling, I can't figure out why God has allowed all this to happen.''

There was a long pause. Then I went on, "It's bad enough that the house hasn't sold. But I've accepted the fact that it won't until God allows it. I don't understand why I'm feeling this separation from Christian friends though." It was such a frustrating period I was going through, and it bothered me that I couldn't figure it out.

I set out to make the best of our situation because I had no idea of how long it would go on. I started taking advantage of my long lunch time on Wednesdays. It was the only day I could plan on having a long lunch period because Dr. Muderspach played racketball on Wednesdays. I usually planned to go to the hospital that day and have lunch with Alice.

This was one way of spending time with my friends. Of course, Alan and I spent a lot of time with Alice and her friend on the weekends, but I still missed the Bible studies.

Now rumors began to fly in the company that Alan worked for. We heard that Alan would be sent to Seattle. He'd be in charge of that area. We didn't count on this, though, because there were so many conflicting rumors and hostilities in management. One week Alan's boss would call him and tell him that it looked good and the next week tell him that it didn't.

Alan and I decided that we didn't care one way or the other. But try as we did to wait patiently, we began to feel like yo-yos, up one moment and down another. We only wished the company would make up its mind once and for all. It went on for a couple of months and was beginning to make us very unsettled even though we tried not to pay much attention to it all.

The idea of being transferred appealed to me, because the company would buy our house and pay all our expenses. It would finally be our chance to get out of debt. However, such a move also terrified me.

What would happen to us spiritually? Although we didn't see as much of our Christian friends as we would like, they were still here and close by if we needed them.

I had gotten quite secure in my own little world with my job and my friends. The thought of moving, leaving my job and friends, and going to a new area where we knew nobody petrified me.

Then Dr. Muderspach would tease by saying, "You can't quit! You can let Alan go and you stay here, or you can commute here. Better yet, I'll accept your notice of resignation if you give me a year's notice."

He would tease me constantly, but admitted, "I'll miss you, Sharon, if and when you leave."

That made me feel important and needed around the office. The thought of moving brought up so many mixed feelings, but slowly the thoughts of being out of debt became more and more appealing.

At last management finally decided to hire someone from the East Coast for the job. Of course we couldn't help feeling a little disappointed.

"Well, at least it's over and we can get back to a normal life not having to worry what's going to happen next," Alan confided in me.

It wasn't over though. Within a few days after the man arrived from the East and started working in the territory, the company changed the commission percentages. The man figured out that with that change he wouldn't make any more money than he had made in the East. He couldn't justify moving his family clear across the country for no more money, so he packed up and went back East.

This left the territory uncovered again. Upper management finally called Alan's boss and said, "Go ahead; do what you want. If you want Alan up there, put him there. We'll start on getting corporate approval for the transfer."

This started our emotions going all over again. We decided that since the house had been on the market for so long and hadn't sold, that we'd just let the company buy it.

A couple of weeks later we got our transfer papers in the mail. We filled out all the forms necessary to expedite the company's buying our house. Then we had to wait four or five weeks for corporate approval for the transfer. Until that came through we decided not to start looking for a new house.

I told Dr. Muderspach that we would probably be moving to Seattle. "It looks pretty definite now. We are waiting for the company's approval on the move."

"Let me know as soon as possible when you'll be leaving so I'll have enough time to replace you, although I'll really miss you around here. You're a good worker," the doctor told me.

I remembered that Debbie, the woman I had replaced, was thinking of going back to work part time, and maybe she'd come to work if the doctor asked her. I told him about Debbie.

"Thanks, that's a great idea. I'll have to talk to her," he answered. Then he added that he and Elaine wanted to take Alan and me out for a farewell dinner.

"That's really nice of you," I said. "But not really necessary. The both of you have been so nice already."

"I know it's not necessary, but we want to do it. I know with Alan working up in Seattle during the week that it leaves only the weekend. You folks are a lot busier than Elaine and I, so just tell us when you can go, and we'll make the arrangements."

Alan at this point was traveling back and forth to Seattle, coming home on the weekends. It went on for a period of three months before we finally moved. It was extremely tiring and hard on all of us.

One day I got to thinking about why the house hadn't sold during the time we had it on the market, my going to work, seeing less of my Christian friends—not having them to lean on every time I had a problem.

It was all becoming clear to me, and I'm sure the understanding was from the Lord.

The Jones's leaving was a blessing! We, especially me, had become extremely dependent on Mike, the pastor. It had almost gotten to the point where Mike was our only connection with the Lord. We had to learn to trust and depend on the Lord, not on any human being. Then came my working and having to stop the Wednesday prayer group, besides not having the time during the day to spend with Doris, who always kept me close to the Lord. That Christian fellowship everyone needs so desperately.

Doris began working part time and had to work the times I had off. So I saw less and less of her. Sometimes weeks would go by, and my only contact with her would be at church.

Finally, it came to me! A year ago we weren't ready to be on our own. We were like babies at a crawling stage, not ready to walk alone yet!

Not until we were willing to deal with our problems instead of running from them, and definitely not until we started depending and looking directly to God for our answers instead of to ministers and friends, did we find ourselves standing alone but in God's strength.

We had to go through a weaning process to prepare us to be on our own, to depend only on the Lord. Once we were able to accept our circumstances as they were, deal with them as responsible Christians, things became easier.

Mike Jones's leaving was the first step of this process, and also the hardest. Alan and I had to learn to pray directly to the Lord and to trust Him, not using Mike as a go-between.

Then, of course, my working, Doris's working, and the Bible studies ceasing were yet other steps of the weaning process. Then and only then were we ready to leave this area and be strong enough Christians to continue to live a good Christian life. We could never give up Bible study and prayer, but we had to learn to depend on God rather than on our friends.

There is a saying I once heard, "It's You and me, Lord, right. You and me!" That's exactly the case with us. We had to reach that point in our Christian growth before we could really appreciate what we were and what we had, and be satisfied.

He had this move all planned long ago, but we weren't ready. We had to be prepared to be able to be on our own. Most times we are so stubborn and impatient, wanting our own way and right now, not wanting to wait.

The Lord always knows the end from the beginning. If we could only learn to be patient and trust Him!

Chapter Seven

Who am I? What do I want out of life? I guess I want the impossible—just to be happy! Is it impossible to have the fruits of the Spirit?

The kind of happiness that probably is in fairy tales, a make-believe kind of love, is not the fruit of the Spirit. A deep kind of love, in which you can sense someone's emotions and moods without words being spoken, a kind of fullness in your life that makes it worth living, a genuine caring and sharing—that is the fruit of the Spirit.

How do you learn to trust enough to be able to personalize Jesus and know that He died for you? Are we worthy enough of that kind of love?

It seems like Christians are always having struggles, when the people of the world seem to have it so easy! Have you noticed that? David, the psalmist, did. Of course, I'm sure it is because the devil has decided to leave them alone. After all, aren't they already in his care? Satan doesn't have to worry about them.

Do you feel afraid? Afraid of what? The responsibility! If I'm alone, I don't have to worry about letting anyone down or trying to live up to someone's expectations of me! Of course, this isn't normal thinking. For a lonely, frightened person who continually refuses to give his life to Jesus, I'm sure, a lot of these feelings and thoughts are something he lives with daily, but believe me, these feelings will all disappear once you learn to trust and love Jesus as your personal Saviour.

Have you ever said, "I just don't know how to be sure of myself or to accept things for what they are! Lord, why do You allow me to feel this way? Why can't You stop it?"

If we could do that and the Lord stepped in and answered our prayer the way we asked, we would probably just sit back and take things for granted and would never strive to better ourselves. Trials are for our own good. It isn't the trial that counts; it's our reaction to it.

My guess is that many people at one point in their lives have asked themselves, Who am I? Where am I going? I know I have. But remember to let the Lord lead you always. He's promised He will—"even unto the end." That's all that matters.

The Lord has blessed me so abundantly since becoming a Christian I don't think I could name all my blessings. We sometimes have a habit of forgetting all the thousands of little things, for some reason, and only remembering the big things. But the Lord has answered all my prayer requests, no matter how small. I want to thank Him over and over!

I know I'll not be able to figure out why so many things happened to me on this earth, but I'll understand when Jesus returns. I have learned that the only one in the whole world you can really trust is Jesus! I praise the Lord for that. He never turns His back on anyone. He never leaves anyone alone or deserts anyone—no matter how wrong he may be. If you want Him, He's there—ready to help. Ask Him and believe His promises. His kind of love takes a special kind of being.

This short story someone shared with me always gives me courage. I'm sure you've read this before.

"One night I had a dream. I dreamed I was walking along the beach with the Lord, and across the sky flashed scenes from my life. For each scene I noticed two sets of footprints in the sand—one belonged to me, the other to the Lord.

"When the last scene of my life flashed before me I looked back at the footprints in the sand. I noticed that many times along the path of my life, there was only one set of footprints. I also noticed that it happened at the very lowest and saddest times of my life.

"I questioned the Lord about it. 'Lord, You said that once I decided to follow You, You would walk with me all the way, but I have noticed that during the most troublesome times in my life, there is only one set of footprints. I don't understand why in times when I needed You most, You would leave.'

"The Lord replied, 'My precious child, I would never leave you during your times of trial and suffering. When you see only one set of footprints, it was then that I carried you!' "

How often we forget the Lord's love and strength and patience.

It seems that whenever things go a little wrong or we don't get our own way, we take it out immediately on the Lord. It wasn't His fault that we muffed things. It's so easy for us to put the blame on someone else.

All the Lord wants is for us to love and believe in Him. Why do we in our human form find it so difficult to trust Him? He knows the end from the beginning. He knows what is best for us. He knows us better than we know ourselves.

If you have ever considered leaving the church or had the feeling that you've been cheated or that life's passing you by, stop it! It's not true or worth considering.

The problems that arise out of being so wrapped up in self and what you want are minimal compared to the joys of everlasting life. We forget our real purpose in life.

Believe me, the more you search for the things you think you're missing in the world, the lonelier and more dissatisfied you will become. No matter how much money you have, how much you smoke, drink, take drugs, or party, you will never have anything satisfactory until you have Jesus in your life.

When you take Him into your life and plans, you will realize just how little you did have and how unhappy you were. There is nothing more fulfilling and exciting than finally giving your life to Jesus.

When you are involved with the things of the world, you become selfish, bitter, impatient, lonely, frightened and feel unloved. But if you just learn to trust in the Lord, all things become possible as He leads with His strength and love.

The excitement of love, self-confidence, the ability to do things you never before thought possible will overwhelm you. All the things you've heard about the strength of the Lord are true, and there are even more. I know I have, I have proved it.

Here is a big challenge. Why not try to win someone close to you to Christ by letting him or her see the new you? Set an example that will be noticed. There is no better feeling than to lead someone to Christ. There is no better way to witness the love of Christ than through your own life, your Christlike life.

Being a new Christian I have had a lot of adjustments

to deal with. The main one was an emotion. I was dealing with feelings that I had been cheated by not being raised an Adventist Christian.

I marvel at the knowledge and understanding Seventh-day Adventists have of the Bible, the excellent hospitals and health programs they have going, their educational system, and much more. The percentage of Adventist children that get a college education in an Adventist college is staggering. Also, after a few visits to any Adventist church it's hard to believe the number of talented people in one building.

A talent in an Adventist child is noted by both parents or even by church members, and that talent is encouraged. Next to the Lord, I feel the most important matter to Adventist people seems to be that their children get the best available, well-rounded Christian education possible.

I am so thankful that my husband and I found the truth while the children are still young enough to take advantage of all that is offered to them.

I truly feel that everything that has happened in my life happened with a purpose—to lead me to Christ. I praise the Lord I allowed Him to lead me. I now have an extremely close relationship and bond that can now never be broken by anyone or anything.

Sometimes people grow lax in their experience. They may take things for granted. Sometimes it takes a tragedy or near tragedy to make one realize his need of the Lord.

I feel so blessed coming into the Adventist religion now after all those things have happened because I feel I can really appreciate this church and its teachings so much better having had to find it on my own.

Who me, Lord? No, I would constantly say, even up to a couple of weeks ago, but I'm not ready, Lord. I don't know that much about the Bible yet that I feel confident witnessing to non-Christians, and I do so often feel inadequate to serve the Lord. But I am learning there are many ways to serve the Lord, and I'm going to do so whenever possible.

One area in which I feel extremely confident to give counsel is in overcoming the cigarette habit. With the total victory over cigarettes the Lord has given me I feel I have to let other people know of His power. They can also have the desire to smoke completely removed if only they will believe and ask the Lord for His help.

I have started to get involved in helping with some Five-Day Plans and hope to have the opportunity to witness to people the love the Lord has for all of us if only we open that door all the way, reach out, and commit ourselves to Him.

I know I now have the acceptance of the most important being, the Friend and Master of the whole universe—the Lord! What more could anyone want!

I know that, from now on, I am going to live my life, which is Christ living in me, not everyone else's. That I am going to ask the Lord to change *me*, not change everyone else to suit me. I am going to take one day at a time, instead of my whole future at once, because we can live only one day at a time. So why add unnecessary burdens to an already difficult world?

I know that I need a daily surrender to the Lord, and I must ask for His guidance. I now have the trust in the Lord to help me live in this world and work for others. And while working for others, I am working for the Lord and developing my own Christian self.

John 14:14 says, "If ye shall ask any thing in my name, I will do it." And in Psalm 32:8, it says, "I will instruct thee and teach thee in the way which thou

shalt go: I will guide thee with mine eye." That
means God never sleeps. His eyes are always open to
our needs. God has never slept in my experiences.
He's always been there and ready to help.

Give yourself to Him. You'll never regret it. Do it
now! Ask Him for guidance. He'll give it. He is an
ever- loving and patient God. He's the same yesterday,
today, and forever.